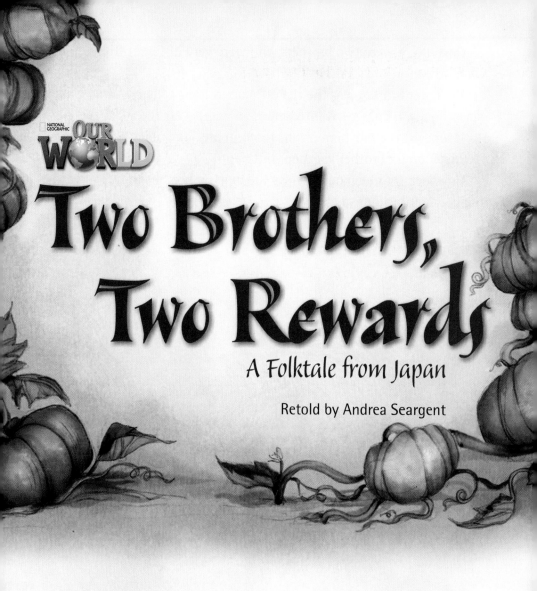

NATIONAL GEOGRAPHIC
OUR WORLD

Two Brothers, Two Rewards

A Folktale from Japan

Retold by Andrea Seargent

T0349309

NATIONAL
GEOGRAPHIC
LEARNING

CENGAGE
Learning

Once there were two brothers who were very different from each other.

The older brother was the richest man in their village, but he was never happy. He always wanted more.

"Money is the most important thing in life," the older brother said.

The younger brother was poor but happy.

"I believe that helping others is the most important thing in life," the younger brother said.

One day, the younger brother found a sparrow on the ground. It had a broken wing.

"Poor bird, you can't fly," he said. "I will help you."

The brother carefully picked up the bird and brought it home. He cared for the sparrow for many days. After a month, the sparrow's wing was better.

"Now you can fly," said the younger brother. "Goodbye, little friend!"

The sparrow didn't fly away. Instead, it started to speak.

"I know you don't want a reward for helping me," said the sparrow, "but please take this small present."

The sparrow gave the younger brother a seed that was in its beak.

"Plant this seed in your garden and take care of it," the bird said.

Then the sparrow flew away.

4

The younger brother planted the seed and watered it each day.

Soon a thick vine grew on the ground. Then, yellow flowers began to bloom. Soon after that, the vine had fat pumpkins on it.

The brother picked a pumpkin for his dinner. But when he cut it open, the pumpkin was filled with gold and jewels!

He cut open more pumpkins. Every one had treasure in it.

The younger brother was now the richest man in the village!

The older brother heard about his brother's treasure.

"No!" he shouted in anger. He didn't like anyone to be richer than he was.

He ran to his brother's house and cried, "How did you get this treasure?"

His brother explained that he helped a sparrow and that the sparrow gave him a magic seed as a reward.

"Then I will help a sparrow, too!" said the older brother. "And I'll get a bigger treasure!"

The greedy brother looked for a sparrow with a broken wing, but he could not find one. So he decided to trap a sparrow.

He put a piece of bread under a box. Soon a sparrow hopped under the box to get the bread. The brother pulled the box down on the bird. The box trapped the bird and broke its wing.

The brother said, "Oh, no! Poor little bird. You are trapped. Your wing is broken! I'll help you."

The greedy brother took the bird home and cared for it. When the bird's wing was better, the brother got ready to let it go.

"But first," said the greedy brother, "you must give me a reward. Remember that I fixed your wing and saved you from that box."

The sparrow said, "Oh yes, I have a reward for you. Plant this pumpkin seed in your garden and take care of it."

Then the brother let the sparrow go.

8

The older brother planted the seed and watered it every day. Soon a thick, black stalk grew. But it didn't grow on the ground like a pumpkin vine. Instead, it went straight up into the clouds all the way to the moon. And it had a terrible odor!

The older brother checked the stalk every day, but no pumpkins grew on it.

"Where are the pumpkins?" he wondered. "It is only a tall, stinky stalk!"

The greedy brother thought, "My treasure must be at the top of this stalk!"

So, he began to climb up the stalk. The odor was so strong, he tried to hold his breath. But he thought of the gold and jewels he would find at the top, and he kept climbing.

He climbed higher and higher until finally, he stepped onto the moon. Just then, the stalk died and fell to Earth.

The greedy brother was stranded on the moon—with no treasure.

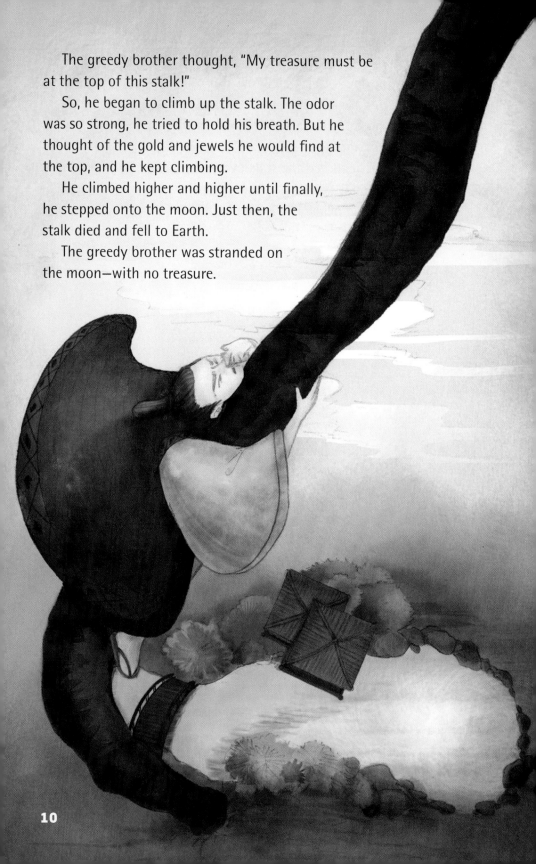

And ever since that day, the greedy brother looks down from the moon once every month. He is still looking for his treasure back on Earth.

Instead, he sees his happy younger brother helping others.

You can see the older brother yourself. Just look up at the moon the next time it is full, and you will see his face. He is the man in the moon, and he's not very happy.

Facts About Amazing Plants

There are about 400,000 different kinds of plants in the world. And some of them are pretty amazing!

Pitcher Plant

Named for its shape (a pitcher is a large container used for holding and pouring liquids), the pitcher plant may collect up to 7.5 liters (2 gallons) of rainwater. Insects love the sweet juice on the leaves of this plant. Once an insect gets inside the plant, it falls into the water the plant has collected, and the insect is trapped. The juice of the plant contains chemicals that slowly dissolve the insect. Then the plant digests the insect.

Pelican Flower

Before its flower opens, this plant looks like a sleeping pelican. Once open, it looks beautiful. However, its smell is terrible. It smells like a dead animal! But this stinky odor brings flies and beetles to feed on this plant.

Watermeal Plant

Watermeal is the world's smallest plant with flowers. It also produces the world's tiniest fruit! This plant is about the size of the head of a pin, and it weighs about as much as two grains of salt! This tiny plant floats on lakes and ponds. It has no roots, so the side of the plant that sits in the water absorbs nutrients.

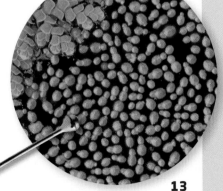

Word Play Plants

Circle the correct word to complete each sentence.

1. The corn (stalk / vine) grew taller each day.

2. We picked the tomatoes right off the (stalk / vine).

3. I saw the most beautiful (bloom / stalk) in the garden.

4. The seeds were planted in the (vine / ground).

5. Most plants absorb (ground / nutrients) from soil.

6. The plant has a terrible (stinky / odor).

7. It smells (stinky / odor).

Write the word for each picture. Then, on a separate piece of paper, write sentences using each word.

ground   vines   bloom   stalks

vines

Glossary

absorbs soaks up

gold a very valuable yellow metal used for jewelry

grains very small pieces, often of food

greedy wanting more than is fair to have

jewels stones that are very valuable

money coins and paper that are used to buy things

poor having very little money

reward a present someone gives someone else for doing something good

richest having the most money

sparrow a small grayish-brown bird

stranded stuck and unable to get down or away from somewhere

treasure a large amount of gold, jewels, or money

wing the part of a bird's body that it moves in order to fly